....

....

....

Hear the upward call of the Master;
Lift your eyes and you will see
New horizons appear,
And the challenge is clear,
Come and climb the heights with me.

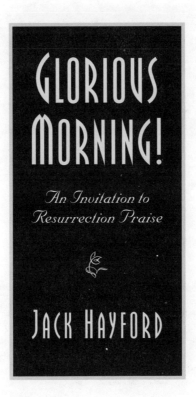

GLORIOUS MORNING!

An Invitation to Resurrection Praise

JACK HAYFORD

MULTNOMAH BOOKS · SISTERS, OREGON

GLORIOUS MORNING!

published by Multnomah Books
a part of the Questar publishing family

© 1996 by Jack W. Hayford

International Standard Book Number: 0-88070-862-X

Cover illustration by Stephanie Henderson
Interior illustration by David Danz
Designed by David Uttley
Edited by Larry Libby

Printed in the United States of America

Most Scripture quotations are from:
The New King James Version (NKJV) © 1984 by Thomas Nelson, Inc.

Also quoted: *The Holy Bible, New International Version* (NIV) © 1973, 1984 by
International Bible Society, used by permission of Zondervan Publishing House

King James Version (KJV)

The Living Bible (TLB) © 1971 by Tyndale House Publishers

The New Testament in Modern English, Revised Edition (Phillips) © 1972 by J.B. Phillips

All songs in this book © Annamarie Music, administered by
Maranatha! Music. Used by permission.

For information write: Questar Publishers, Inc.
Post Office Box 1720, Sisters, Oregon 97759

96 97 98 99 00 01 02 03 — 10 9 8 7 6 5 4 3 2 1

CONTENTS

CELEBRATE THE EMPTY TOMB

ACKNOWLEDGE THE EVIDENCE

RECOGNIZE HIS PRESENCE

RECEIVE HIS LIFE

LIVE IN HIS POWER

GLORIOUS MORNING!

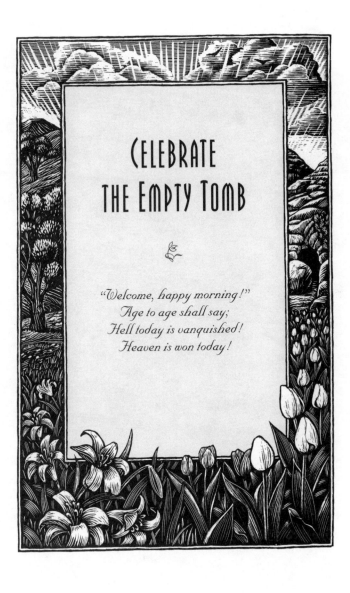

Celebrate the Empty Tomb

"Welcome, happy morning!"
Age to age shall say;
Hell today is vanquished!
Heaven is won today!

GLORIOUS MORNING!

"He is not here, but is risen!"

LUKE 24:6

It's Resurrection Morning, and it is glorious!

What else can you say about Easter?

There's no way to tinsel it. Gifts aren't necessary. Romantic cards aren't appropriate. Lights strung on the garage can't illuminate it. And listen...firecrackers are pip-squeaks compared to the earthquake roar of a stone rolling back from the tomb.

There's nothing louder than life!

There's nothing more glorious than resurrection.

"Celebration" is a diluted, overused word, and I weary of it. *But what else can you say about Easter?* The word was made for the day. The act fits the occasion like a diamond fits an engagement ring.

Yes, celebrate!

Sing, shout, laugh, dance, praise, do cartwheels if you can, but most of all...lift your voice on high. Proclaim majesty!

JESUS CHRIST IS LORD...RISEN INDEED, AND HIGH ABOVE ALL!

Would you come and stand beside Him, with me, in His triumph?

What triumph is that, you ask?

Triumph over Fear

No shadow of fear can withstand the brilliance of the Son-rise. All other shadows of the flesh's limits must fade as well: doubt, pride, lust, hate, habit, and bondage to self.

Anyone who can handle death as effectively as Jesus has is more than adequate to conquer anything that assails me! As Son of God and Son of Man, Jesus effectively merges both spheres — God's infinite power and humanity's infinite need.

Jesus is Lord over weak flesh — even yours and mine! Do you believe it?

Jesus is Lord over failure — even ours! Will you receive it?

Triumph over Religiosity

Call it what you will: ceremonialism, dead-beat memories of churchianity, plastic piety, stained-glass habit, supernaturalistic unrealism, weirdo-fanaticism. The unbounded reality of His life burns through all that like a summer sun piercing a thin mist.

Anyone so almighty as to smash the gates of hell, and so human as to invite weary, doubting men to breakfast with Him, is my kind of Savior. John chapter 21 reminds me that

He's demanding enough to expect my allegiance but patient enough to help me grow in full discipleship. Jesus is Lord above "religious" methods of salvation.

Triumph over Tomorrow

Jesus is Lord over life's question marks — over uncertainties, over seasons of confusion and disorientation, over ignorance about where I'm headed. All these piled up clouds of anxiety are scattered to the winds by the wild, sweet cry of joy that echoes through the centuries: *He is alive! He is risen as He said!*

Anyone who can descend into death, conquer hell and the devil, touch bases with earth and earthlings, and then spring heavenward into the glorious rule at the right hand of All Power on high deserves my vote of confidence about handling my future — and whatever *it* holds.

They said of Him at Pentecost that it was not possible that death could hold Him. Nor can it restrain us who hold His hand.

Join me, friend, in trumpeting a celebration offered to every man and woman from every corner of our bruised and battered planet. Let's worship the Risen One together. It's a joyous occupation that will engage us through the bright eons of eternity with the redeemed of all ages and all heaven's angels.

We might as well get a jump on it now.

Amen! And Hallelujah!

A SHEPHERD'S CALL TO NEW HEIGHTS

"My sheep hear My voice . . .
and they follow Me."

JOHN 10:27

Spring is the season the shepherds call their sheep to leave the lowlands and begin to climb the heights. Winter snows are past, and the mountains spread their carpet of verdant beauty. Fresh grass, sprays of flowers, and blossoming trees beckon upward.

Come, My flock. Rich feasting and fulfilling growth await if you follow Me to the heights.

Hear the upward call of the Master;
lift your eyes and you will see
New horizons appear,
and the challenge is clear,
Come and climb the heights with me.
Never let your heart be shackled
by affections earthly bound.
Follow Christ today
up the narrow way
That leads to higher ground.

A synonym for spring is Lent, an old English word for this bright season of newness. It is also a religious term which denotes the Lenten observances of self-denial, which many Christians have traditionally practiced during the forty days preceding Easter. Like many traditions, Lent has suffered the decay that seeps into and eventually destroys valid habits when they are not understood, or when the vital spirituality that birthed them has withered.

I strongly believe that in approaching Easter and the glorious days preceding — Palm Sunday, Maundy Thursday, and Good Friday — we should require something special of ourselves.

These days should not go by as ordinary.

The classical term "Holy Week" may sound archaic and coldly liturgical. But what our Lord Jesus did in those eight days has forever changed history — and each of our lives.

Jesus Himself calls us upward — to abandon the hazy lowlands, to climb the heights, to move on to fresh, rich pastures of His purpose for our lives. So, here are some "sheep paths" I'd like to suggest, ways to heed His call as Easter approaches:

ONE: Pick a book of Scripture, preferably one of the Gospels, and make a commitment to read it all the way through in these few days leading to Resurrection Sunday. Make space for what the Holy Spirit can do in you as His truth makes you free.

TWO: Make a point of inviting at least two couples or singles into your home, or out for coffee, during these Lenten days. Attempt to reach out to people in your congregation who are not part of your usual circle of friends.

THREE: Set aside the ten days leading to Easter as *ten days of triumph*. Allow Him to help you focus on one personal discipline that you renew or begin to refine into steadfast practice, using every day until Easter Sunday to establish this.

A life of resurrection victory awaits us all — here and now! Loved one, there is more than flowers and trees that's intended to blossom this springtime. *Life* is breaking out all over. Let's all welcome its nearness and go upward and forward together.

Jesus Christ Is Alive!

But God raised him from the dead . . .
because it was impossible for death
to keep its hold on him.

ACTS 2:24, NIV

I t was early autumn, not springtime.

It was in the plains of South Dakota, not a garden in Jerusalem.

It was 1976, a long time after that first Easter.

I was riding a bicycle on a little, graveled road through a graveyard, pushing a rigid exercise regimen — hardly the setting for the birth of an Easter anthem. But it happened.

Suddenly my spirit leaped with inner joy. The landscape of tombstones and memorials sprawling across the expansive lawn seemed to ignite a triumphant strain.

"Jesus, Jesus, Jesus Christ is alive!"

There wasn't anyone to hear my song being born, but within five years, choirs across the nation would join in the simple refrain begun in a cemetery:

Jesus, Jesus, Jesus Christ is alive!
Jesus is alive — King of kings!

Jesus, Jesus, Jesus Christ is alive!
  Because He's alive I can sing!

For the death which could not contain Him,
    it cannot conquer me;
And the power of sin is broken,
    and my spirit is now free,
      to sing that
Jesus, Jesus, Jesus Christ is alive!
  Jesus is alive forevermore!

Jesus, Jesus, Jesus Christ is alive!
  Jesus is alive — King of kings!
Jesus, Jesus, Jesus Christ is alive!
  Because He's alive, trust His words.

You shall live just the same as I live,
    and I'll never forsake.
Flood or flame shall not overwhelm you;
    all the way I will take you
      through to
Glory, Glory, Jesus Christ is alive!
  Jesus is alive forevermore!

It's years behind me, now. But I don't think I'll ever forget that bike ride. It was more than the birth of a song. It's a constant reminder that any season, any place, and on any terms, the joy and power of the Savior's life-gift to us and in us is timelessly available and irresistibly overcoming.

Sing it out!

Easter: A New Order

*Just as he was raised from the dead
. . .so we too might rise to life on a
new plane altogether.*

ROMANS 6:4, PHILLIPS

he chaotic, the run-amok, and the pointless are traits of our time. Consider the relentless parade of activities, the incessant flood of mail, the endless ringing of telephones, and the stream of requirements, adjustments in procedure, refinements of policy that flow to you from your superior at work.

Students face assignment piled on assignment.

All of us endure a barrage of information, entertainment, and miscellany that keep our eyes glued to the TV tube lest we miss something. A dozen new magazines a week suggest you subscribe to keep abreast of what's really happening.

The modern American preoccupation with being contemporary, informed, and socially "with it" drives most of us toward a life of whirlwind confusion. Gadgets expedite the performance of all our essential duties. Speed-read courses help us weather the storm of print sweeping upon us. Plans to systematize our day, week, month, or year and other "hurry-up-and-get-it-done-right" techniques are upon us ad infinitum.

In the midst of it all, the police whistle of my soul screams its shrill command — HALT!

It is only as I stand there, mentally gasping for breath, that I discover how tired I have become…how much I want to stop. Not to stop living, but to stop rushing. Not to retreat from reality, but to reenter life.

Looking up, I discover where the call of my soul has brought me to a complete stop: at Jesus' empty tomb.

Step in with me, and as we rejoice in the triumph of His resurrection, let us learn from one detail there.

When Peter and John looked into the empty tomb, they found the graveclothes Jesus had left, neatly folded. The carefully arranged graveclothes and linen napkin described in John 20:4–28 suggest a new order at the Resurrection. The explosion of life that burst the bonds of death has a simple system to it. Step inside the closed tomb, and with your imagination watch the body of Christ begin to breathe. See the Son of God sit up, remove the headwrap, and methodically disrobe Himself from the cloth-chains which symbolize man's final futility. The garments are neatly placed at the spot where He removes each. And as you look, you see Him clothed by garments not of earthly origin — garments which will be worn later that day as He comforts a tearful woman, as He hikes to

Emmaus with two troubled disciples, and as He dines that evening with the men closest to Him.

So many applications are there for our understanding. But rather than draw them all, just pray with me, would you?

Lord Jesus, let the new order of life which You opened to me reign over me. Clothe me with Your unhurried, not-stampeded-by-urgency mindedness. Let the powerful simplicity of Your order and control characterize my heart, my home, and my hopes.

Making a Big Deal of Easter

*So they went out quickly from
the tomb with fear and great joy, and ran to
bring His disciples word.*

MATTHEW 28:8

I came across a phenomenon sometime back, a peculiar expression by some sincere Christians who felt it was "unspiritual to make a big thing out of Easter."

In fact, they reacted so much to the traditional practice of big crowds, much music, high rejoicing, and dressing up that they refused even to go to church on Easter (though they did go most of the year).

While I didn't agree with them, I wasn't particularly irritated. I took it all with a shrug of the shoulders and a to-each-his-own and it-takes-all-kinds sort of allowance for their peculiarity.

But the more I thought about this, the more I became convinced that they were not only wrong but they were victims of a deadly kind of reactionary spirit. It stirred me to press all the more for a bold, loud, forthright, festive, and celebrative Easter.

Why do I recommend this sort of thinking?

First, because it's consistent with the Bible.

The angel at the tomb said, "Go quickly and tell His disciples" (Matthew 28:7). The obvious reason is to spread the word. Tell everybody. And be quick about it. Don't sit on Good News. This is a day above all days!

Then on Easter night, after their first encounter with their resurrected Master, the Word says: "Then the disciples were *glad* when they saw the Lord" (John 20:20, my emphasis).

The whole spirit of the day is to spread the word to more and more. Crowds are the idea! And gladness should be *everywhere*. It's in the Book.

Second, because it's simply logical.

Since death has been vanquished, the more lively our celebration the more appropriate to the occasion. No wonder so many people dress up with new clothes on Easter. While some may attack that practice as a social "carnal parade," I hold that new Easter outfits are just one more way to say, "New life is here, and I'm celebrating the newness!" Jesus had new clothes on Easter, too!

Third, because a "big" Easter should summon prayerful preparation among the Lord's people.

At least two reasons make this appropriate:

• The Good Friday lead-in to Easter's weekend is a heart-sobering time of humbling our souls and reflecting on the Cross of Christ — the inestimably high price of our immeasurably grand salvation.

• Easter Sunday is a unique occasion to invite people to

church…and to Christ. People will more likely visit church with you on this day than any other, and we ought to reach toward and pray for their spiritual openness.

Fourth, because the very thought of the Resurrection should fill the skies with our songs of triumph!

Jesus Christ has burst forth from the tomb and the open door of the grave shouts like a song-filled mouth: "Christ is risen! Rejoice! Rejoice!" If *that* doesn't make you want to celebrate this Easter, it's time to ask for a resurrection of your own!

ACKNOWLEDGE THE EVIDENCE

Angels in bright raiment
Rolled the stone away,
Kept the folded graveclothes
Where Thy body lay.

No more we doubt Thee,
Glorious Prince of Life!
Life is naught without Thee;
Aid us in our strife.

Many Infallible Proofs

"Reach your hand here, and put it into My side.
Do not be unbelieving, but believing."

JOHN 20:27

uke the physician, one of the most respected, verifiably reliable historians to pen accounts of ancient events, opens his record of the early church by stating:

Jesus…also presented Himself alive after His suffering by many infallible proofs, being seen by them during forty days…. (Acts 1:1–3)

As a man of scientific inquiry, this medical doctor who wrote the Gospel that bears his name, opens his historic narrative of the *continuing* manifestations of Jesus' *ongoing* life and ministry by establishing essential grounds for credibility.

In other words:

Jesus is still believed in,

still followed,

still working His mighty, miraculous works.

Why? *Because He who died is alive again* — the Son of God, our Savior!

In every generation — from the day of the Resurrection when the soldiers who witnessed it were paid to lie about what they had seen — there have been those who stoutly deny Christ's resurrection. Some denials are simply that: a flat refusal to believe. Other denials through the years have taken on a misty, flowery, poetic form. We hear talk of "the continuation of an influence" or "the persistence of a Christ-idea that rises freshly in our hearts like the flowers of spring." Whatever form the Great Lie takes, it remains what it is: the knee-jerk reflex of hell itself. Unable to quench the truth, it moves to dilute or distort it.

But as the centuries pass, inescapable evidence of Christ's undeniable reality verifies itself in the life and experience of multiplied millions of tough minds, as well as tender hearts.

Luke the historian wouldn't have been satisfied with anything less than verifiable facts.

Thomas, the hard-nosed cynic, wouldn't have been stirred by philosophy or poetry.

The disciples, whose dreams of earthly Messianic glory were shattered at the bloody Cross on Mount Calvary, would have never — *could* have never — pulled off a high-minded religious charade.

• They would have never regrouped…after running in fear for their very lives.

• They would have never believed…after watching their first ideas of Jesus' purpose and mission explode into a million pieces.

• They would have never boldly preached the gospel of His life, death, and resurrection.

• They would have never laid down their very lives — as witness to His reality — unless…unless…UNLESS…

Jesus Christ was alive, and they knew it!

They staked their lives on Reality, not a mental invention, a phantom experience, or a gush of sentiment. Don't make any mistake: the apostles were tough-minded men — a mixture of hard-working, clear-thinking guys who came to their conclusions independent of one another. There were no "soft sells" in the bunch, and yet all of them, having seen and spent time with the resurrected Lord, set the course of their lives to declare the triple truth:

• Jesus of Nazareth is the Messiah;

• Jesus is the Son of God, Savior of the world;

• Jesus' resurrection proves the above is true.

The record of God's Word reveals at least a dozen post-resurrection appearances of Jesus, with up to as many as five hundred people being present at once. Watch as Scripture ticks off its witnesses. Who saw Him after His resurrection?

1. *The two women* — *Matthew 28:5–10*

2. *Mary Magdalene* — *John 20:11–18; Mark 16:9*

3. *The two disciples en route to Emmaus* — *Luke 24:13–35; Mark 16:12–13*

4. *Peter (Cephas)* — *1 Corinthians 15:5*

5. *The Ten* — *Luke 24:36–43; John 20:19–24*

6. *The Eleven (Thomas present)* — *John 20:24–29*

7. *The Seven in Galilee* — *John 21:1–19*

8. *The Eleven again (in Galilee)* — *Matthew 28:16–18*

9. *The Five Hundred* — *1 Corinthians 15:6*

10. *James* — *1 Corinthians 15:7*

11. *Paul* — *1 Corinthians 15:8*

In addition to these, there were the witnesses to His dramatic ascension (Acts 1:1–11). General references to His ongoing teaching ministry after His resurrection (Acts 1:3) suggest repeated, lengthy times of presence with people, making clear that the undeniably *dead* Jesus was now unmistakably *alive!*

Let the record speak! He answered skeptics, ate with those who at first feared He was a ghost, and was touched by and spent extended time with real people *as a real person.*

To this day, this same resurrected Jesus satisfies the doubts of honest inquirers all over the world. As we enter into Easter worship to His praise and in His honor, we forthrightly declare with Peter, "We did not follow cunningly devised fables…but were eyewitnesses of His majesty" (2 Peter 1:16).

We have stepped into the light of the solid facts of the Resurrection, and we can see —

Jesus is Lord,

forgiveness of sins is ours,

and heaven is our eternal home with Him!

Alive Forevermore!

*I am He who lives, and was dead,
and behold, I am alive forevermore."*

REVELATION 1:18

There aren't any like Him — like Jesus, that is!

There is a lot of talk these days about life beyond life, about reincarnation, about contact with some "cosmic consciousness," and miscellaneous other mutterings of human inquiry into the invisible.

But with Jesus, you have a different case. Entirely. Definitely.

Jesus is the only person in history who died and came back *permanently*. The "behold" is an old-fashioned way of shouting, "Check this out!" He is saying, "Look here!" And the conclusion of history adds, "Look *only* here!"

Why? Because looking for life outside of Jesus the Son of God is like looking for the sun after cutting off your head. He's the only One who came back from the dead so conclusively. Not just for twenty minutes or twenty years; His is a resurrection, not a resuscitation. His everlastingness — His endless quality of life — is a commentary on the Source from which it flows. He was raised by the power of *God*. And that transcends by eons anything a paramedic can do.

And in saying, "I am alive forevermore," He adds, "and I have the keys of death and hell." In short, there is no force or fury that can conquer your life when you place yourself in the hands of the living Lord.

Look! And live!

RECOGNIZE HIS PRESENCE

Show Thy face in brightness,
Bid the nations see;
Bring again our daylight;
Day returns with Thee!

All Resurrections Are Not the Same

*Now if we died with Christ, we believe that
we shall also live with Him.*

ROMANS 6:8

ot every resurrection is the same…but everyone can
share the same resurrection.

Jesus wants us to understand how His resurrection
life works for us. While He walked on earth, Jesus
raised three people from the dead prior to His own victory
over the grave. Though the end result — life! — was the same,
each was unique.

Jairus's Daughter

She was twelve years old, and she had just died. Her body,
perhaps still warm, lay on the same bed where she had passed
away. The crowd of professional mourners had only just begun
their noisy fluting and wailing. Jesus looked into the shocked,
anguished eyes of Jairus, her father, and held them for a
moment. "Do not be afraid," He said, "only believe" (Mark
5:36).

Taking the girl's mother, father, and three of His closest

disciples, Jesus went into the room of death and looked down at the petite body so recently vacated by its young tenant.

> Then He took the child by the hand, and said to her, "Talitha, cumi," which is translated, "Little girl, I say to you, arise."
>
> Immediately the girl arose and walked.... And they were overcome with great amazement. But He commanded them strictly that no one should know it, and said that something should be given her to eat. (Mark 5:41–43)

The Widow's Son

> When He came near the gate of the city, behold, a dead man was being carried out, the only son of his mother; and she was a widow. And a large crowd from the city was with her. When the Lord saw her, He had compassion on her and said to her, "Do not weep." Then He came and touched the open coffin, and those who carried him stood still. And He said, "Young man, I say to you, arise." So he who was dead sat up and began to speak. And He presented him to his mother.
>
> Then fear came upon all, and they glorified God. (Luke 7:12–16)

A woman at that time and place who had no husband or son was at the economic mercy of the society — and would be reduced to begging. Jesus understood the situation. Unlike Jairus's daughter, this young man had probably been dead for a day or two. The procession to the tomb was already in progress when Jesus encountered it, interrupted it, and transformed the funeral party into a *real* party.

Lazarus

Jesus arrived *four days* after Lazarus had died. Mary and Martha, the dead man's sisters, were crushed with disappointment and grief. Each in her turn greeted Jesus with the words, "Lord, if You had been here, my brother would not have died." Was it a simple statement of fact, or was there some bewilderment and mild reproach in the statement? It was as though they were saying, *Lord, where were You? What we needed from You was a quick healing, and what we got was delay!*

Gently, Jesus turned the issue from one of mere timing to one of essential relationship.

Jesus said to her, "I am the resurrection and the life. He who believes in Me, though he may die, he shall live. And whoever lives and believes in Me shall never die. Do you believe this?"
(John 11:25–26)

Martha affirmed her belief in an end-time resurrection, but Jesus was saying, "I'm talking about *now*, Martha."

The central issue wasn't whether Lazarus would be raised from a sick bed or a grave. The issue wasn't whether Lazarus would be resurrected sooner or later…in four minutes, four hours, four days, or four millennia. The issue was where — and in Whom — resurrection life was centered.

"Late" or not, Jesus arrived at Lazarus's tomb and ordered that the stone be rolled away from the opening.

> *Martha, the sister of him who was dead, said to Him, "Lord, by this time there is a stench, for he has been dead four days."*
>
> *Jesus said to her, "Did I not say to you that if you would believe you would see the glory of God?" Then they took away the stone from the place where the dead man was lying.… [Jesus] cried with a loud voice, "Lazarus, come forth!" And he who had died came out bound hand and foot with graveclothes, and his face was wrapped with a cloth. Jesus said to them, "Loose him, and let him go." (John 11:39–41, 43–44)*

All resurrections are not the same.

Sometimes God steps in instantly, as He did with Jairus's daughter. We've all found ourselves in situations that looked hopeless and futile. Yet we cried out to Jesus, and *instantly* something happened. Instantly something of God's divine grace and power penetrated our darkness. I've heard person after person say, "I thought we were dead for sure, but we called on the Lord, and He stepped in immediately."

Sometimes, however, He chooses not to answer on the instant. Sometimes He waits. The widow of Nain encountered her miracle a day or more after her son had died. She might have said, "Lord, if You had been here, my son would never have died at all, and I wouldn't have experienced all of this grief." But I seriously doubt there was even a shadow of complaint on her heart. He who is Life had intersected her path, lifted her grief, and returned her son — laughing and alive — to her arms again.

In the case of Lazarus, however, the funeral procession had long since passed by. He was already in the grave. The body wasn't only stone cold, it was decaying. Yet Jesus, facing a tomb much like the one in which He would be laid just days later, called His friend back from beyond.

No, all resurrections are not the same. But those who belong to Jesus share the same resurrection life. His life. It is a life that will ultimately cancel the sting of death and usher us into heaven. But it is also a life that touches us *today*.

Jesus isn't so much asking about your faith in a future resurrection; He's asking if you believe His life can penetrate the death that claws at you *now* — in any part of your daily experience.

The shadow of death is something we must contend with every day of our lives. David described it like this:

The pains of death surrounded me.
And the pangs of Sheol laid hold of me;
I found trouble and sorrow.
Then I called upon the name of the LORD:
"O LORD, I implore You, deliver my soul!"
(Psalm 116:3–4)

In order for us to receive the flow of Christ-life and experience release from the bondage which wounds us, limits us, and cripples us, we need to come to a point where we say, "Lord, I believe Your resurrection power toward me as it applies to this situation, *right now.*"

As we do, the words Jesus spoke to Martha that day in Bethany have equal force in our lives as well.

"Did I not say to you that if you would believe you would see the glory of God?"

A Statement Unswerving

*May I never boast except in the cross
of our Lord Jesus Christ.*

GALATIANS 6:14, NIV

was amazed and wounded.

One of my former teachers had written me, for whatever reasons, accusing me from his posture of retirement and accumulating years: "You are unfaithful to the Word. You have forsaken the Cross."

Stunned, I turned to Dr. Bird, my first bishop after my entrance into ministry and a father to me in the faith. At seventy-eight years of age, he was a better judge of what was being said by one of his peers.

"Jack," he consoled, "don't worry. Your ministry stands firm on the Rock of Ages. Perhaps this dear brother is just losing touch."

I knew that my old friend and teacher was aware of my *heart* at least. But I felt my *words* needed to be clear, too. I had to write to him, but I needed to be gentle with a beloved man of senior service in Christ. Paul was clear on that score when he wrote to his young colleague in the ministry: "Do not rebuke an older man, but exhort him as a father" (1 Timothy 5:1).

Ever so carefully I composed an answer to my former teacher, enclosing the following lyrics from a hymn I had recently penned. I wrote: "Please take time to judge from this what Christ, His Cross, and God's Word mean to me."

Teach Me about Thy Cross

Teach me about Thy Cross, dear Lord,
　　nothing presumed, I've all to learn.
Spirit of God, unfold the Word;
　　Thy deepest secrets let me discern.

Prone to indulge my selfish whims;
　　failing to learn Thy purity;
Bent on my will, my pride, my sins;
　　teach of Thy Cross, and liberate me.

Make of Thy Cross a yoke for me;
　　crowd me toward life, all sin erase.
Discipline every energy,
　　Lord, may Thy glory shine on my face.

Jesus, Thy Cross all pow'r has gained;
　　sin, death, and hell now vanquished lay.

May I by faith that vict'ry claim,
    and in Thy triumph reign every day.
Nor earth nor hell can e'er compete;
    I am now loosed, who once was bound.
Serpents and scorpions 'neath my feet;
    Christ's conq'ring glory shines all around.

I eventually came to terms with my old mentor. But as the years have gone by, I've become increasingly convinced that wherever two or more human beings gather, Misunderstanding slips in as the uninvited guest. That's why I find such comfort clinging to the unshakable truths of Easter — truths that cannot be altered, diminished, or diluted by the passage of time or human follies and frailties.

- God's Word is TRUE,
- Christ's Cross is SUFFICIENT TO SAVE, and
- JESUS IS LORD.

Let us come to His Cross again today, unmistakably assured in the salvation it affords, and unswerving in our commitment to Him…and His Cross.

In a world where no piece of ground seems secure, this is our sure and unshakable Rock.

The Doorways of Easter

*"I am the door. If anyone enters by Me,
he shall be saved."*

JOHN 10:9

ow many doors open into the radiant truth of Easter? As I've mused over the last few weeks, three come to mind.

There was a shaken door…at a doorway to a tomb.

There was a shared door…at a doorway to an inn.

There was a shut door…at a doorway to an upstairs room.

The first door was shaken by an angel and an earthquake. The second door was shared by two friends who invited a strangely familiar, fellow traveler in for a meal. The third door was shut by a small band of men, desperately fearful of reprisals.

All of these doors pertain to Easter. And each represents the difficulty we have in facing a miracle. Everybody *wants* a miracle, but when it happens, we don't know how to handle it. We don't know what to do with it. We end up searching for some "logical" explanation.

Upon closer examination, each of these doors — the three doors of Easter — speaks to a basic human need.

The Shaken Door

Now after the Sabbath, as the first day of the week began to dawn,…behold, there was a great earthquake; for an angel of the Lord descended from heaven, and came and rolled back the stone from the door, and sat on it. His countenance was like lightning, and his clothing as white as snow. And the guards shook for fear of him, and became like dead men.

But the angel answered and said to the women, "Do not be afraid, for I know that you seek Jesus who was crucified. He is not here; for He is risen, as He said. Come, see the place where the Lord lay. And go quickly and tell His disciples that He is risen from the dead, and indeed He is going before you into Galilee; there you will see Him. Behold, I have told you."

So they went out quickly from the tomb with fear and great joy, and ran to bring His disciples word.

Then Simon Peter came…and went into the tomb; and he saw the linen cloths lying there, and the handkerchief that had been around His head, not lying with the linen cloths, but folded together in a place by itself. (Matthew 28:1–8; John 20:6–7)

It wasn't an earthquake that rolled that massive stone from the door; it was an angel. And it wasn't to let Jesus out, because He had already vacated the premises! The Resurrection was already history, and the mighty angel threw open that door to show an empty tomb.

John and Peter ran to the tomb, and — as was his way — Peter barged right in. Scripture meticulously describes what he found there — vacated graveclothes, and a neatly folded handkerchief that had once covered the face of a dead man. *But where was the corpse?*

Peter and John were both astounded at what they saw, though Peter was slow to accept the dramatic evidence in front of his own eyes. He hesitated, wanting to believe, but hardly daring to believe.

What was he seeing? The work of vandals? Grave robbers? What grave robbers would carefully remove those linen graveclothes and fold them neatly within an empty tomb? There was undeniable evidence here of rational, practical, ordered activity.

Why did Peter hesitate to believe? Did he still feel heavy with the shame of denying his Lord? Did he find himself thinking, as songwriter Don Francisco suggests, *Even if He is alive, it wouldn't be the same?*

Peter's crushing sense of failure and betrayal shadowed everything he saw that bright resurrection morning.

I wonder if we feel the same way sometimes. I wonder if some of us hesitate to respond to the message of Easter because of embarrassment and shame over past failures. We don't feel like celebrating because we're all too conscious of our own weakness and failure. We don't feel worthy to enter into such pure and exalted joy.

Yet the empty tomb boldly declares that if death has been conquered, there is *nothing* that can ultimately defeat you. Whatever would press in upon you, whatever insistent voices might whisper words of doubt and despair in your ear, you may take your stand at the shaken door. With an empty tomb behind you, you may say with confidence, "By the resurrection power of Jesus Christ, nothing — not even death in all its forms — can ever defeat me."

> *If the same Spirit that raised Christ from the dead dwells in your body, He will bring God's life and power into every part of your present experience.* (Romans 8:11, my paraphrase)

The Shared Door

Now behold, two of them were traveling that same day to a village called Emmaus.... So it was, while they conversed and reasoned, that Jesus Himself drew near and went with them. But their eyes were restrained, so that they did not know Him....

Then they drew near to the village where they were going, and He indicated that He would have gone farther. But they constrained Him, saying, "Abide with us...." And He went in to stay with them.

Now it came to pass, as He sat at the table with them, that He took bread, blessed and broke it, and gave it to them. Then their eyes were opened and they knew Him. (Luke 24:13, 15–16, 28–31)

Anna and I have walked a portion of the road to Emmaus. There is a section of that ancient Roman highway — perhaps 150 yards long — still intact, though surrounded by rubble. It was deeply moving to tread the very stones where, two thousand years ago, two others walked with sad faces and heavy hearts. And then — suddenly — there were three. At some point in their journey Cleopas and his companion were joined by a third traveler, one whom they should have recognized, but somehow didn't.

Later, the two men would marvel at how moved they'd felt when the Stranger walked them through the scrolls of holy writ and taught them about the living Christ. "Were not our hearts burning within us while he talked with us on the road and opened the Scriptures to us?" (Luke 24:32, NIV).

When they arrived in town, they invited their Companion in for some refreshment. They simply opened the door to the Lord Jesus, and He walked right in. As they gathered around the table, their Guest broke the bread, and the Bible tells us: "He was known to them in the breaking of the bread" (v. 35).

Wherever you may be, in whatever situation you may find

yourself today, Jesus will step right in as you open the door to Him. He will enter with salvation. He will enter with healing. He will enter with strength, and counsel, and matchless wisdom. Whether you realize it or not, whether you recognize Him or not, He has been traveling with you on your long and winding journey.

It's time to invite Him in for a meal.

"Behold, I stand at the door and knock. If anyone hears My voice and opens the door, I will come in to him and dine with him, and he with Me." (Revelation 3:20)

The Shut Door

Then, the same day at evening, being the first day of the week, when the doors were shut where the disciples were assembled, for fear of the Jews, Jesus came and stood in the midst, and said to them, "Peace be with you." When He had said this, He showed them His hands and His side. Then the disciples were glad when they saw the Lord....

And after eight days His disciples were again inside, and Thomas with them. Jesus came, the doors being shut, and stood in the midst, and said, "Peace to you!" Then He said to Thomas, "Reach your finger here, and look at My hands; and reach your hand here, and put it into My side. Do not be unbelieving, but believing."

And Thomas answered and said to Him, "My Lord and my God!" (John 20:19–20, 26–28)

Jesus entered twice, it says, with "the doors being shut." His visits were a week apart. The first was Easter night, scarcely hours after His resurrection. The next was eight days later, the following Sunday. And in each case, He bypassed locked and bolted doors to be with His dear friends. Imagine! The greatest single event in world history had just taken place on their very doorstep, and the disciples shut the door! Twice!

Shut doors so often tell the story of our relationship with the Lord. Each of us has the terrible capacity to slam the door in the face of God's promises...not just His promise for salvation and eternal life, but His promises for our lives, for our families, for our businesses, for our relationships, for our weaknesses, for our torment, for our bondage.

It wasn't so much that these disciples intended to shut God out; they had simply allowed a deep fear to shut them in. In Thomas's case, a paralyzing doubt kept him locked up tight. Yet in spite of all the barred doors and shuttered windows, Jesus suddenly stood in their midst and said, "Peace be to you."

God's love is relentless. We lock ourselves up in anxiety, distress, perplexity, and grief, and Jesus moves right into our situation, shut doors and all. He is in no way reluctant to walk right through our deepest confusion and despair.

The key to the doorways of Easter is in the recognition that your first reaction need not close you out of coming to a right response. However you may have responded in days gone by, it is your response *now* that matters to God.

Do acknowledge the evidence.

Do recognize His presence.

Do receive the grace that will not allow you to shut the door in the face of His powerful, life-building promises.

Follow me now through the doorways of Easter. Jesus is saying, "Let's walk through them together."

Jesus, Now Thy Power Displaying

Jesus, now Thy power displaying,
Changeless Savior e'er the same.
In my days as yesterday
Be strong to magnify Thy Name.
Jesus, Jesus, stand beside me,
Prove the wonder of Thy power.
Sin abounds and hell assails me,
Now Thy grace the more o'ershower.

Jesus Christ, Thou Son of David,
Heal the blind and lift the lame.
Now as then in Galilee
Stretch forth Thy hand, exalt Thy Name.
Jesus, Jesus, resurrection
Power and life distill from Thee
As at Laz'rus' tomb now call,
Destroy the curse and set me free.

Jesus, Son of God now crying,
"Not my will but Thine be done."
My Gethsemane surrounds me;
Keep me an obedient one.
Jesus, Jesus, I would follow

In the triumph of Thy pain.
Vict'ry after vict'ry winning:
Life is Christ and death is gain.

Jesus, Master of the tumult,
You who calmed the troubled sea;
Over-billowed, swept and storm-tossed,
Weary I repair to Thee.
Jesus, Jesus, rise from slumber,
Still the raging tempest here;
Shout and silence screaming demons,
Quell my heart from doubt and fear.

Jesus, Jesus, King of Glory,
Come again as ne'er before.
Once a Lamb, now come a Lion,
Let all hell now hear Thy roar.
Quick upon Thy prey now falling,
Strike down evil, purge all sin.
As the sunrise, shed Thy healing
'Til all nations enter in.

(THESE LYRICS MAY BE SUNG TO BEETHOVEN'S "ODE TO JOY.")

Mandatory Nine Count

Wait on the LORD; Be of good courage,
And He shall strengthen your heart.

PSALM 27:14

I can't number the times I have wished God would hurry up…with an answer to my prayer…with a bailout in the middle of my muddle…with a fresh sense of His working in my life.

But there is one well-established principle in the Scriptures, and it is dramatically demonstrated in Jesus' experience.

You can't rush a resurrection.

Matthew's Gospel records at least three times that Jesus clearly prophesied He would be killed by His adversaries and He would rise again (16:21; 17:23; 20:19). He not only stated precisely that it would be the third day, but He predicated His resurrection upon an Old Testament type: the third-day deliverance of Jonah from the belly of the great fish (Matthew 12:40).

These advance notices of His resurrection are forceful arguments for Jesus' sense of purpose and power. They also offer a valuable lesson for you and me. If I am walking in the simple path of God's will for me, *I can never be conquered by anything.* I may be down, but I'm not out. He will get me up again, and He says when it will be…on the count of three.

Have you ever seen a boxer, flattened by his opponent, try to scramble to his feet too quickly? Rather than taking the nine count, using the time to recover his equilibrium, he attempts a quick bounceback. It's as though he's trying to convince himself, the crowd, and his opponent that he isn't *really* hurt. A downed boxer's identity seems wrapped in his ability to show a can't-hurt-me facade, when, in fact, his hurried rising leaves him wobbling, staggering, and open prey for a quick kill at the hand of his competitor.

Consider with me, friend: If Jesus could have called for angels to spare Him the suffering of the Cross (Matthew 26:53), don't you know that He could have called for an early deliverance from death? The message of His submission to the Father's timing as well as the Father's plan is profound in its application to your life and mine.

Don't attempt a humanly energized "bounceback" from those circumstantial "knockdowns" you encounter. God has His own kind of "mandatory nine count": It's a third-day rising for everyone who will wait for His moment of miracle deliverance.

"Easy to say, Pastor Jack, but I've waited longer than three days, or three weeks, or three months…in fact, more than three *years*. What about my resurrection?"

I hear you. And I know the pain often wrapped in that kind of inquiry. But the answer is in a return question: "Have you entrusted everything concerning your case to Jesus?" If you have, then the entire matter is sealed and delivered…in His resurrection.

The message is this: As surely as Jesus rose on time, your triumph will be on schedule also.

Lazarus's schedule probably seemed a day late to him, too.

Great Deliverance, Mighty Redemption

Once in all hist'ry,
O great the myst'ry
God came to earth veiled in flesh
    so man could see.
In Christ the Savior,
God showed His favor
    He to redeem us ascended Calvary.

CHORUS:
Great deliverance!
Mighty redemption!
That can reach the lost like me,
Cleanse from guilt and set me free.
So I'll shout, "Hallelujah!"
And, "Praise God Jehovah!"
For that great deliverance and great victory.

Dark was the hour,
Hell-born the power
Which tore the flesh of the Lamb
    spent on the Tree.
Death now partaking —

Hell's power breaking —
Hear "It is finished!"
>   *The Lamb cries, "Victory!"*

Come to the Mountain —
Bathe in the Fountain,
Wash in the blood Jesus shed
>   *upon that Cross.*
Call Jesus' Name now —
Come make your claim now;
He'll break your bondage,
>   *redeem your every loss.*

CHORUS:
Great deliverance!
Mighty redemption!
That can reach the lost like me,
Cleanse from guilt and set me free.
So I'll shout, "Hallelujah!"
And, "Praise God Jehovah!"
For that great deliverance and great victory.

A Very Strange Easter to You

They glorified God and were filled with fear, saying,
"We have seen strange things today!"

LUKE 6:26

I have to chuckle at the number of people who want God to be predictable.

It is "not fair" for God to act suddenly, powerfully, dramatically, or conclusively. These folks would have Him prepackage life in molded plastic wrapping so that they could look at each issue *before* the fact and decide whether they want to embrace it or not.

Easter is God's answer to this symptom of human fear. In the resurrection of His Son, God is making an explosive declaration that we're not only ignorant of His boundless power, we're also ignorant of the limitless creativity of His *method*.

Who would have expected the Resurrection? The answer in Scripture is clear: no one. Even those Jesus told specifically and clearly in advance were caught off guard.

How could He have stated it any plainer?

*"The Son of Man...will be delivered to the Gentiles and will be
mocked and insulted and spit upon. They will scourge Him and
kill Him. And the third day He will rise again."*
(Luke 18:31–33)

He told them, but they didn't listen. We're all that way.
We'll only hear of the expected. We may wish for or dream of
the unexpected, but if God tells us it's going to happen, we
either doubt it or fear it. We think He might not do what He
has said. Or we're afraid He will. And He says He will. Listen.

*For the Lord shall rise up as in mount Perazim, he shall be
wroth as in the valley of Gibeon, that he may do his work, his
strange work; and bring to pass his act, his strange act.* (Isaiah
28:21, KJV)

This promise is a potent commentary on God's unpre-
dictability. The word *strange* doesn't mean "bizarre" or "weird."
The Hebrew word used in this text means "unusual," or "coming from an unexpected source."

The examples given by the prophet illustrate the point.
"Mount Perazim" refers to the occasion in which God gave
David a dramatic victory by breaking forth like a flood tide
over the adversaries he faced. The "valley of Gibeon" refers to
the day the sun stood still in the heavens to afford Joshua and

his army the opportunity to conclude their triumph over their enemies. Both cases speak of victory in adversity.

And both were strange. Unusual. Unpredictable.

• As unpredictable as winning a battle you don't actually fight, in which the enemy is swept from your path by a tidal wave of God's power rolling out ahead of you.

• As unpredictable as the sun standing still. That's strange, friend, strange.

But not as strange as the dead's rising.

That's the strangest of all. Empty graves are in a league of their own. Jesus' resurrection categorically *excludes* any hopelessness in any situation and *includes* anyone who opens to His life-gift. This is something more than life beyond death; it is life beyond hope. God's declaration that He shall "rise up" and work an unusual deliverance is ultimately confirmed and manifested in the resurrection of Jesus. When hope fades, life expectancy can rise again. When shadows crowd you, expect the unexpected.

Easter is the evidence that such expectations are reasonable.

Resurrection Chorus

Sing the resurrection chorus,
Jesus is alive!
Christ has died and risen for us,
Jesus is alive!

CHORUS:
Jesus is alive!
Jesus is alive!
Jesus is alive, alive forever.
Jesus is alive!
Jesus is alive!
Jesus is alive forever more.

Hell is crushed, death's door is broken,
Jesus is alive!
Calvary's victr'y here is spoken,
Jesus is alive!

Sing aloud and shout the message,
Jesus is alive!
Jesus opened heaven's passage,
Jesus is alive!

Come receive His great salvation,
Jesus is alive!
Jesus opened heaven's passage,
Jesus is alive!

Lift your hands, exalt Him ever,
Jesus is alive!
Thus we'll worship Him forever,
Jesus is alive!

The Seekers and the Stone

*"Who will roll away the stone
from the door of the tomb for us?"*

MARK 16:3

s the three women walked along in the predawn twilight, they knew they had a very large problem. They
were facing a physical impossibility, and none of them
had any idea what she was going to do about it.

But still they came.

The stone that had been rolled across the mouth of Jesus'
tomb was larger and heavier than three women could possibly
manage. For that matter, it may have been more than three
brawny men could have tackled.

They came anyway.

The stone had been sealed by Rome, the greatest world
power ever known to that day. A contingent of soldiers had
been placed in front of the stone, guaranteeing that no one
would gain access to the tomb.

Still, the women approached.

The great stone reminds us of those seemingly insur-
mountable troubles and questions in our lives: our difficulties,
weaknesses, habits, dependencies, family stresses, relationship

problems, physical or emotional pain. We find ourselves wondering how we will ever solve them. In our honest moments, we acknowledge that we will never be able to face them or answer them or move them in our own wisdom and strength.

• The stone in the garden was real, just as our problems are today.

• The stone in the garden was enormous, just as our personal difficulties loom in our minds and cast a shadow across our souls.

• The stone in the garden was under constant armed guard, just as we are beset today by the powers of Satan and demon darkness.

But we can learn from these three women; they can teach us how to approach a barrier bigger than we are. Note how they came.

They came hopefully.

They had seen in Jesus the fulfillment of their highest dreams. Everything they had anticipated in connection with those hopes had been dashed to fragments in the shadow of the blood-soaked Cross. The natural human response to that reality would have been, "Why should we do anything anymore? Why bother? It's been three days, and the tomb has been sealed by Caesar's army."

Nevertheless... "Very early in the morning, on the first day of the week, they came to the tomb when the sun had risen."

They didn't know what would happen. They didn't know what to do. They didn't know who might help. But everything they had learned about Jesus of Nazareth since they had first met Him taught them to come expectantly.

How do you approach a "great stone" in your life? You choose to come with expectation. Hope is a starting place. You choose to open your heart to hope in the face of any and all physical barriers.

They came humbly.

Now when the Sabbath was past, Mary Magdalene, Mary the mother of James, and Salome brought spices, that they might come and anoint Him. (Mark 16:1)

They came to serve Him — in death as in life. They came reverently, to do what they could for Him. They hadn't been able to shield their Lord and friend from the unjust charges and the sham trial. They hadn't been able to protect His body from the savage beatings, the humiliation, and the Cross. But what they *could* do, they surely would do. They came with reverence, humility, and gentleness of heart to care for His broken body.

Two chapters back, in Mark 14, we read what Jesus said of another devoted woman, who had broken an alabaster flask of costly ointment and poured it over His feet. Some who were present hadn't valued that service, and criticized her sharply.

> But Jesus said, "Let her alone. Why do you trouble her? She has
> done a good work for Me.... She has done what she could.
> She has come beforehand to anoint My body for burial.
> Assuredly, I say to you, wherever this gospel is preached in the
> whole world, what this woman has done will also be told as
> a memorial to her." (Mark 14:6, 8–9)

That woman did what she could before His death, to prepare His body. In the same way, the women who approached His tomb after the crucifixion were humbly doing what they could out of love for Him. That's all the Lord asks of us, isn't it? We do what we can, we do what's in our power, and then in humility, we leave the impossibilities to Him.

They came helplessly.

Humility, however, doesn't come naturally! There's something in our flesh that rises up and insists we want to do it "on our own." We want to give it our best shot, we want to give it all we've got — and then call on God later if it isn't enough. As these women approached the stone, they asked among themselves, "Who will roll the stone from the door of the tomb for us?" It was a fundamental acknowledgment that they couldn't do it themselves. We need that same acknowledgment in our lives, too. Jesus said, "Without Me you can do nothing" (John 15:5). That's not an insult; it's just a statement of plain fact.

If we want to see large obstacles move in our lives, we must come to a point of honest admission. We can do nothing about them. Our best efforts will not avail. Positive thinking and visualization will accomplish exactly nothing. If anything is to be done, the power of the Living Christ must accomplish it.

What happened then, when the women reached their destination?

> When they looked up, they saw that the stone had been rolled away — for it was very large. And entering the tomb, they saw a young man clothed in a long white robe sitting on the right side; and they were alarmed.
>
> But he said to them, "Do not be alarmed. You seek Jesus of Nazareth, who was crucified. He is risen! He is not here. See the place where they laid Him. But go, tell His disciples — and Peter — that He is going before you into Galilee; there you will see Him." (Mark 16:4–7)

When they reached the stone, it had already been rolled away! When they reached the tomb, there was no body! Their problems and questions had already been solved by the resurrection of the Lord Jesus.

That's where our answers lie as well, and nowhere else. The

resurrection of Jesus Christ has rolled away that which blocks our future, making possible the entry into what God has for every one of us.

And entering the tomb, they saw...

They saw life in the place of death! They saw heaven's messenger in the place of hopelessness and corruption. When those early seekers looked into the tomb, they found their questions already answered, their needs already met.

The call of God's Word is timeless. Look and live! Let *us* look to the same empty tomb to find it has removed all obstacles to our tomorrows.

You will never need to worry about moving tomorrow's "large stones" if you'll let Easter happen where you are today.

All Is Well

Raised by hate upon a hill,
Stark there stands a Cross of wood.
Look, the Man they take and kill,
Is the Lamb, the Son of God.
See the blood now freely flow;
"It is finished," hear Him cry!
Who can understand or know,
Death has won; yet death will die.

CHORUS:
All is well, all is well,
Through Christ our conq'rer, all is well!
All is well, all is well,
Through Christ our conq'rer, all is well!

Slashing wounds now scar the Lamb,
Blemish-free until He's slain.
Hammerblows into His hand,
Thunder forth again, again.
See His body raised in scorn,
See the spear now split His side!
Yet the vict'ry shall be won,
By this Man thus crucified.

Look! The Cross now raised on high,
    Symbol of Christ's reign above.
Cow'ring demons fear and fly,
    Driv'n before the flame of love.
All of hell is mystified;
    Satan thought this hour his gain.
See God's wisdom glorified:
    Death destroyed in Jesus' name.

Here is hope in hopelessness;
    Here is joy where all is pain.
Here a fount of righteousness
    Flows to all who make their claim.
Come and drink here, Come and live;
    Come and feast on life and peace.
In the Cross God's all He gives;
    In the Cross is full release!

Tow'ring o'er all history,
    Stands the Cross of Christ the King.
Crossroads of all destiny,
    At the Cross is ev'rything.
See here death hung on a Cross,
    See self slain upon a tree,

See disease and ev'ry loss
Overthrown through Calvary!

CHORUS:
All is well, all is well,
Through Christ our conq'rer, all is well!
All is well, all is well,
Through Christ our conq'rer, all is well!

RECEIVE HIS LIFE

The cross He bore is
life and health,
Tho' shame and death to Him:
His people's hope,
His people's wealth,
Their everlasting theme.

Your First Day of Forever

*Whoever hears my word
and believes him who sent me has eternal life . . .
he has crossed over from death to life.*

JOHN 5:24, NIV

My father died over ten years ago, and some would say that was his first day of forever.

But it isn't so.

Yes, on that day in August, Daddy went to be with the Lord. On that day he left us for heaven, going to the place Jesus had prepared for him.

But it wasn't his first day of eternal life.

My father's well-thumbed Bible rests on the desk of my study at home. If you were to open it to the first page, you would see these words penned in blue ink:

Jack William Hayford, Sr.
On October 27, 1935, I received eternal life.

It was in an evening service in a little church in Long Beach, California. The pastor preached on a text from the book of Revelation:

And the Spirit and the bride say, Come. And let him that
heareth say, Come. And let him that is athirst come. And who-
soever will, let him take the water of life freely.
(Revelation 22:17, KJV)

He and my mother took God at His Word. Both of them
came to Jesus that night. And some time that night before he
went to bed, Dad recorded the date and wrote down what had
happened to him.

That was my father's first day of forever. And my own first
day of forever came about ten years after that.

Eternal life, you see, is more than *duration* of life, or length
of time.

It's more than some ghostly, ethereal experience that happens to you "after you die."

It's more than going to heaven and experiencing eternal
utopia.

It's more than "that part of me that continues even after
I'm gone."

These notions sound good, but when you bring them
down into the push and pull of daily living, they really don't
cut it. And when you hold them up to the Word of God, they
fade in the blazing light of a greater truth.

The only absolute authority on the subject, Jesus Christ, has the final word:

"And this is eternal life, that they may know You, the only true God, and Jesus Christ whom You have sent." (John 17:3)

What is life eternal? It is meeting, knowing, and joining ourselves in relationship to God the Father, and His Son, Jesus Christ. It is experiencing the power of His resurrection life — not just in the sweet by-and-by, but in the nasty now-and-now.

Scripture says that He brought life *and* immortality at His appearing.

…our Savior Jesus Christ, who has abolished death and brought life and immortality to light through the gospel.
(2 Timothy 1:10)

Immortality has to do with our forever future.
Life is what is happening here and now!

It is a quality of life never before possible for the children of Adam and Eve. It is life of the highest potential, possibility, and expectancy. It hints at a nobility and beauty beyond the reach of normal human experience. That is the life introduced to us through Jesus Christ and made possible by His resurrection on that first Easter morning.

Paul expressed it in these stunning words:

*I have been crucified with Christ: and I myself no longer live,
but Christ lives in me. And the real life I now have within this
body is a result of my trusting in the Son of God, who loved me
and gave himself for me. (Galatians 2:20, TLB)*

Christ lives in me! This is eternal life. And what is the quality of that life?

• We could speak of His love, without measure.

• We could speak of His forgiveness, beyond comprehension.

• We could speak of His healing touch, like no other.

• We could speak of His shattering victory over death and
Satan.

Eternal life begins the moment you acknowledge Jesus
Christ as Savior and Lord.

It's too big to wait until forever.

Worship Christ, the Risen King

Rise, O Church, and lift your voices.
Christ has conquered death and hell.
Sing as all the earth rejoices;
Resurrection-anthems swell.
Come and worship, come and worship,
Worship Christ, the Risen King!

See the tomb where death had laid Him,
Empty now, its mouth declares:
"Death and I could not contain Him.
For the Throne of Life He shares."
Come and worship, come and worship,
Worship Christ, the Risen King!

Hear the earth protest and tremble.
See the stone removed with pow'r.
All hell's minions may assemble
But cannot withstand His hour.
He has conquered, He has conquered,
Christ the Lord, the Risen King!

Doubt may lift its head to murmur,
Scoffers mock and sinners jeer;
But the truth proclaims a wonder

Thoughtful hearts receive with cheer.
He is risen, He is risen,
Now receive the Risen King!

We acclaim your life, O Jesus.
Now we sing your victory.
Sin or hell may seek to seize us,
But your conquest keeps us free.
Stand in triumph, stand in triumph,
Worship Christ, the Risen King!

(LYRICS MAY BE SUNG TO THE MELODY OF "ANGELS FROM THE REALMS OF GLORY.")

More Than a Savior

Our great God and Savior Jesus Christ,
who gave Himself for us, that He might redeem us.
TITUS 2:13,14

illed with drama and emotion, the biblical book of
Ruth tells the story of a young woman who lost
everything but her will to trust in God. It concludes
with her marriage to a man named Boaz, whose
principal role in Ruth's life is defined in a single word: *redeemer*.

The purpose of this piece of history being included in the
Bible may have been to describe the entrance of a Gentile
woman into the ancestral bloodline of the Messiah. But students of the Bible see an even grander lesson.

Here is great insight into God's ways of dealing with ruined
people. Here is the picture of the "kinsman-redeemer" — a
role and relationship God gave under the Old Covenant in
order to help us understand His ways under the New.

The kinsman-redeemer law stated that if someone lost his
possessions through the death of a loved one, another one of
his "kin" could volunteer to repossess that which was lost
(Leviticus 25:24–25). The kinsman's "redeemer" role was

fulfilled in two ways: (1) he had to acknowledge his relationship with the one who had suffered loss; and (2) he had to pay the required price for the recovery of what had been lost.

In the case of Boaz's redeeming actions toward Ruth, he became both a rescuer and a restorer. Ruth was a foreigner and alien in a new cultural environment. Boaz received this disenfranchised widow as his wife and graciously secured her future through restoration of property she otherwise would have lost.

The power of this story transcends its immediate beauty, emotion, and historical significance. Its force emerges in its dynamic picture of what Jesus Christ has done and will do for everyone who puts his or her trust in Him. Jesus is the Savior, but He is even more than that! He is more than a Forgiver of our sins. He is even more than our Provider of eternal life. He is our Redeemer! He is the One who is ready to recover and restore what the power of sin and death has taken from us.

It is a mighty truth, worthy of our deepest understanding. Here's how He does it.

He acknowledges us.

The kinsman-redeemer pictured in the Old Testament had to step forward in open declaration of his relationship to the individual who had been shamed, embarrassed, or ruined by loss or failure. Just as Boaz responded to Ruth's appeal for help, the

Lord Jesus Christ has fully come to us as a kinsman. "The Word became flesh and dwelt among us" (John 1:14). God became "kin" to mankind! He took upon Himself the form of a servant and was made in the likeness of men (Philippians 2:7), fully demonstrating His willingness to associate with us — even though we have sinned against Him. He who never sinned at all was willing to be invested with our sin in order to become our Sin-Bearer and Savior (2 Corinthians 5:21).

But having become "one of us," He went one step further. He personally acknowledges a relationship with each of us: "He is not ashamed to call each of us His brothers — His sisters — His very own family" (Hebrew 2:11, my paraphrase). No matter how badly we have failed, no matter how far we have fallen, we are not beyond His reach. Nor will our sins prevent Him from willingly identifying with us. He has become our Kinsman, and He is ready to claim association with any who will come to Him.

He paid the price.

The word *redeem,* as used in the Bible, describes "a price that has been paid." In the pawnshop usage of the term, a broker gives a "redemption ticket," which a person may use to reclaim something he has sold for far less than it's worth.

This "pawnshop" image provides a dramatic picture of the

way sin works in human lives, tempting us to sell out for less than God's promised blessing, and leaving us with little or nothing as a reward. Yet, as with the rules of the "pawnshop redemption," recovery occurs when a greater price is paid for redeeming what had been "sold cheap" and lost. And that is what Jesus did as Savior:

> *In Him we have redemption through His blood, the forgiveness of sins, according to the riches of His grace.* (Ephesians 1:7)

> *You were not redeemed with corruptible things, like silver or gold...but with the precious blood of Christ.* (1 Peter 1:18–19)

Everything Jesus offers of new life, new hope, and new possibilities is guaranteed to us on the basis of a total and complete payment.

He brings full recovery.

Few realize the thrilling truth that Christ's payment for our redemption involves an ongoing, continual process of recovery! The significance of this provision is clearly apparent when we assess the destructive impact of sin and failure on the human personality.

How many have suffered loss because of sin!

So many have been injured, broken, and damaged.

People are so often left as emotional, physical, and mental casualties through human failure.

The failure may not even be one's own. Damaged people are often the result of someone else's neglect, exploitation, or violation. On the other hand, the loss may be the individual's own just due, resulting from conscious rebellion or defiance toward what he or she knew to be right. Nevertheless, the wreckage wrought in any of our lives may be mended as surely as the sin may be forgiven.

The precious truth of Jesus' power as Redeemer is that He has a plan and an ability to restore progressively the broken parts of human experience and to reproduce a whole person. His salvation is not only an act of forgiveness, it is also a progressive action of redemption. He notably meets us at the moment of our new birth, but His saving life generates a momentum which can bring us into the fullness of restored life and joy.

There is no dearer truth in the Word of God than this: Christ is "able to save to the uttermost those who come to God through Him" (Hebrews 7:25). That simply means that in the recovery process, there is no distance too great for Him to bring us.

God said to the farmers of ancient Israel, "I will restore to you the years that the swarming locust has eaten" (Joel 2:25).

In those words He prophesies a promise answering our present need as well. Whatever has been decayed or destroyed, He is our Restorer-Recoverer-Redeemer!

Whatever your loss, pain, failure, or brokenness, Jesus Christ is fully capable of bringing about change unto full restoration. Just as His resurrection power brings new life, His redemption power brings new hope. He is able, for He's more than a Savior! He's your Redeemer who promises that He will give "beauty for ashes, the oil of joy for mourning" (Isaiah 61:3).

So just as you gave Him your heart and received Him as Savior, give Him your life's broken pieces. Receive Him as Redeemer. Give Him time to work a full redemptive recovery in each part of your life. Let these promises be set in motion as in childlike faith you receive His commitment to restore everything sin has damaged, lost, or ruined.

Begin now to praise Him! You will discover that worshiping Him in this light leads out of the darkness of all despair over sin's effect and aftermath. Let redemptive power and life flow as you praise Jesus Christ — your Savior, your Redeemer, and your Risen Lord!

A Friday's Remembrance

This day I come to celebrate
The day You died to consecrate
A race forlorn;
Which, 'til You came,
Was without hope or champion.

You came — what incongruity!
God is man; eternity
Confined to time
That men might be
Renewed to live in dignity.

To reconcile, a battle plan
Is laid to purchase peace.
You spanned the chasm
Carved by sin;
Your Cross-quake
Closed the breach between.

That Friday has named this one "Good."
How can it be?
We spilled Your blood!
What guilt!

Yet, "Good," I hear You say.
"My new creation birthed this day."

While birth pangs break Your body there,
On Calvary, my stripes You wear.
Your wounded hands,
Your heart,
Your side
Are flowing, Lord, a healing tide.

And so this day's remembrance —
Remembering, remembering:
The cost
The Cross,
The Christ — God's Son.
Lord Jesus, it's to You I come.

I come to take, I come to drink
Again of grace,
And here I think
What great salvation You afford:
I've been redeemed,
Returned, restored!

I live again because You died,
Partake the feast Your love provides;

I break Your body,
Take Your blood,
While seated at Your table, Lord.

This leper — clean!
This blind man — sees!
Your Cross the doubly healing key
Now freeing me from death's decay;
Now flooding life with endless day.

Jesus Meets a Realist

Taste and see that the LORD is good;
blessed is the man who takes refuge in him.

PSALM 34:8, NIV

I'd like to know God," the young man told me, "but — I don't know how."

His name was Phil, and he told me that even though he wanted to believe, he really didn't believe.

"That's OK, Phil," I told him. "Don't worry about that. But let me suggest something here. Would you be willing to pray a prayer with me?"

"I don't know if I can...."

"That's all right. I'll tell you what to say."

So I prayed, and Phil (unsure but willing) repeated after me: "God, I don't even know if You're there. But I do ask You this, sincerely from my heart, that if You will somehow show Yourself to me, I'll serve You with all my heart."

Phil said thank-you and went on his way.

That same evening he walked into a restaurant by himself, was seated, and started scanning the menu. A few minutes later another man walked in and took a seat near Phil. They began to talk, and Phil noticed that the man was carrying a Bible.

"That's strange," he said.

"What's strange?" the man asked.

"Well, it's strange that you would walk into this restaurant and sit down here with that Bible. Just a couple of hours ago I prayed a prayer. I said, 'God, if You're real, please show Yourself to me.' It makes me a little nervous to think that — maybe — that's what you're doing here."

The man not only had a Bible, he had a testimony. He took the opportunity to tell Phil about his relationship with Jesus Christ. Phil still wasn't ready to make a decision. It all seemed too strange. But after a few days of thinking about it, he made up his mind. He gave his life to Jesus Christ.

Jesus has a way of meeting people where they are. Jesus met Phil where he was, in his doubt and unbelief. And that's exactly where he met Thomas, too.

To this day we call him "Doubting Thomas." But he was really just a tight-fisted realist. Hard-nosed. Naturally skeptical. Cautious. The type of individual that gives salespeople fits. No one ever accused Thomas of being from Missouri, but that "show me" attitude was certainly in evidence.

When Jesus told the disciples they were headed back to Judea at one point in His ministry, Thomas was at his pessimistic but loyal best:

Then Thomas, who is called the Twin, said to his fellow disciples, "Let us also go, that we may die with Him." (John 11:16)

Some time later, when Jesus began explaining some deep spiritual realities at the Last Supper, it was Thomas who wanted to bring it all down to a flat, practical, bottom line.

Jesus said:

"In My Father's house are many mansions; if it were not so, I would have told you. I go to prepare a place for you. And if I go and prepare a place for you, I will come again and receive you to Myself; that where I am, there you may be also. And where I go you know, and the way you know." (John 14:2–4)

I can just visualize Thomas holding up his hand at this point and saying, "Lord, wait a minute here!"

Thomas said to Him, "Lord, we do not know where You are going, and how can we know the way?" (v. 5)

Thomas wanted to get it straight. He wanted it in plain Aramaic. He wanted to know the plan. He wanted to see it on a chart and a map.

The night of the Resurrection Thomas wasn't present when the other ten disciples met and spoke with their risen Lord.

Thomas heard the report — *verified by ten of his close colleagues* — but refused to "get his hopes up" until he had further evidence. He told his friends:

> *"Unless I see in His hands the print of the nails, and put my finger into the print of the nails, and put my hand into His side, I will not believe."* (John 20:25)

Just a week later the risen Jesus Christ hand-delivered that evidence to Thomas in the same upper room where He had appeared before.

> *Jesus came, the doors being shut, and stood in the midst, and said "Peace to you!" Then He said to Thomas, "Reach your finger here, and look at My hands; and reach your hand here, and put it into My side. Do not be unbelieving, but believing."*
>
> *And Thomas answered and said to Him, "My Lord and my God!"* (John 20:26–28)

This is an encounter between the squint-eyed realist and the Ultimate Pragmatist, because Jesus is very practical. I weary with the portrayals that paint anything to do with God, Jesus, and the Bible as some kind of ethereal, mystical, poetic sort of impractical concept that you can't isolate and get your hands on.

Jesus was willing to meet Thomas exactly where he was.

Realist to realist. "Put your hand here, Thomas. Put your finger here. Touch Me. Stop wavering in unbelief and get on board!"

Again and again I've seen the hand of God reaching into the most practical details of His children's circumstances. I've seen Him meet men and women in their doubt and perplexity. I've seen Him answer the specific prayers of honest seekers. The Lord says to us, "I know the things you have questions about and doubts about, and I will address them directly if you'll ask Me to."

He's ready to meet you right where you are — *wherever* you are — if you will reach out your hand and put it into His outstretched hand. When you think about it, He didn't only meet us halfway, He came all the way from heaven to earth to prove and demonstrate His great love.

That's evidence enough, friend.

Even if you're from Missouri.

LIVE IN HIS POWER

*I know that
my Redeemer liveth,
And on the earth again shall stand;
I know eternal life He giveth,
That grace and power are
in His hand.*

Christ Has Risen, He's Risen Indeed

Christ has risen!
He's risen indeed!
Conquered death
Its prisoners freed.
Risen now, the eternal seed
Sown to die,
Now alive,
With life overflowing.

Christ has risen!
Forevermore
Broke the seal
And opened the door.
Now He lives
His life to outpour
Over all,
Hear His call,
To life overflowing.

Christ has risen!
He's risen indeed!
Neither death nor hell
Can impede.

His almighty pow'r
Can free.
Come and bow,
Ask Him now,
For life overflowing.

Christ has risen!
Has risen indeed!
Death is dead
Through Calvr'y's tree.
Life is given to you
And me.
Lift your voice,
Now rejoice,
In life overflowing.

Christ has risen!
He's risen on high.
Hallelujahs
Fill all the skies.
All creation joins in the cry
Christ is king,
Ever sing,
Of life overflowing.

HIS NAME IS HIGHER

*Do they not blaspheme that noble name
by which you are called?*

JAMES 2:7

Each Palm Sunday we are ushered back in time to recollect the first time a crowd rose to declare, "JESUS is the CHRIST!"

That's what the stir was about. When the people shouted, "Hosanna to the Son of David!" it meant one thing: This man is the King — the Messiah — the Christ! Jesus of Nazareth is the King above all.

I heard the words "Jesus Christ" uttered several times the other day, but not once were they consistent with the spirit of the Palm Sunday utterances. "Gee-zuz KRIST!" they all said. They meant "Jesus Christ," but from blasphemous lips the name comes out as venom-frozen hatred, anger, or irritation.

We're surrounded by this violation of our Lord's glory and worthiness. It isn't simply a matter of porno literature or X-rated movies, barrooms and brothels, and foul-mouthed mechanics. Jesus is profaned in PG-rated films, in best-selling novels, by the ladylike secretary at the next desk, by the high school honor student next door.

I was tired of wincing. And yet I said nothing. It wasn't a matter of cowardice; I simply lacked conviction that words of correction would accomplish anything worthwhile. In fact, I often wonder if the blasphemer even hears himself.

Sitting in my room, alone, I struggled in prayer: *Lord, I hurt over this hateful habit that pervades my culture. I hurt for these people who mindlessly, ignorantly speak Your name in hate, anger, and frustration. Help me think, Lord. Help me understand, and help me love aright, as You do — in spite of the blasphemy.*

He answered me with two deep impressions upon my soul.

The first: I suddenly saw that in a strange, reversed way, the blasphemy was a kind of self-incriminating acknowledgment of the majesty of Jesus' person. Nobody appealed to any other name to register his angered wish that whatever was grating him would be different. No one spoke the name of any of the founders of the world's religions. No one snarled out the name of Mohammed, Buddha, or Joseph Smith. No one cursed the name of a relative. No one indicted the government.

Why? Because the basic purpose for blasphemy is to register discontent with some frustrating fact, actually damning its presence. And if one is to do that, one must appeal to an authority who is adequate to overwhelm any fact on earth.

I know that none of those who were misusing our Lord's

name were analyzing this, but the fact remains. Jesus Christ's name is spit out as an epithet a billion times a day, but the day will come when God Almighty will catch the blasphemer by the words of his or her own lips. "You appealed to My Son's authority ten thousand times in your lifetime — but not once did you acknowledge His rule in your heart."

The other impression was simply this: Since the world around is so bold to profane His name, let us be at least as bold to praise it.

He is the Lord — JESUS CHRIST!

The Resurrection Dimension

He will give you, through his great power,
everything you need for living a truly good life.

2 PETER 1:3, TLB

hen Jesus said, "Because I live, you will live also,"
He was declaring a new dimension of life available
to any who will receive Him and His.

Most believers in Jesus live an inferior quality of life
simply because they have never come to terms with His full
offer. Christ the Lord, the resurrected Son of God, has made
available to us both forgiveness of sins *and* fullness of life.
Forgiveness comes when we receive Him as Savior; fullness
comes when we receive the offer of His life.

The Good Friday dimension of life says, "Christ died for
my sins." I believe that, and I receive the payment He made for
my sin. I acknowledge the penalty He suffered as a result of
my wrongdoing. But that does not teach the full measure of
provision which God has made possible through the redeeming work of our Lord. There is a resurrection dimension of life
also, and it is wrapped in the words of Romans 1:

The gospel of God...concerning His Son Jesus Christ our Lord,
who was born of the seed of David according to the flesh, and

declared to be the Son of God with power according to the Spirit of holiness, *by the resurrection from the dead.* (vv. 1, 3–4, my emphasis)

This passage clearly tells us that it was through the power of the Holy Spirit that Jesus was raised from the dead.

That Man who strode forth from the tomb twenty centuries ago is still speaking today: "Because I live, you will live also" (John 14:19).

Look closely now. Those words are not only a promise of an endless life in the glory of God's presence, they hold a guarantee of a present life in the glory of God's power. Jesus is telling you and me that we can move out of the limits of mere human resources for living into the dimension of the Holy Spirit's resources for our living.

Today I invite you where Christ invites you: to live in the resurrection resources of the Spirit-filled life. Romans 8:11 says this is the present and fulfilling potential that awaits each of us who will receive Christ's life-power (fullness) as well as His love-power (forgiveness): "But if the Spirit of Him who raised Jesus from the dead dwells in you, He who raised Christ from the dead will also give life to your mortal bodies through His Spirit who dwells in you."

Step to a new plateau! Let's stand together in the full possibilities of Jesus' life working in us. The resurrection dimension is no twilight zone of mysticism, but a real, practical, and powerful dynamic for life in the here and now.

Victory

Through the long night of my soul
Hope has lost ev'ry goal,
Seemed to dissolve —
All my resolve for Tomorrow was vain.
Then a voice filled my night,
"There's a choice, there's a light.
Look up unto Me
For I'll set you free
And restore you again."
Then I lifted my eyes to the Cross raised on high
To the Mount of Deliverance
To Christ crucified.
Jesus' blood broke my chains,
Jesus' name made me whole
Bringing victory — life and victory to my soul.

Is your heart filled with despair?
Weighted down — every care
Seems to increase, banishing peace as it deepens your pain.
Hear this song in your night
If you long for the light,
"Look up unto Me
For I'll set you free

And restore you again."
So just lift up your eyes to the Cross raised on high
To the Mount of deliverance
To Christ crucified.
Let Jesus' blood break your chains
And Jesus' name make you whole
Bringing victory — life and victory to your soul.

BREAKTHROUGH

The law of the Spirit of life in Christ Jesus
has made me free from the law of sin and death.

ROMANS 8:2

Jesus Christ came to earth to die.

And when He did, He drained death of all its power to contain mankind. He not only paid the penalty of human sin and broke the bondage imposed by the Serpent's grip, but He exploded death's power to intimidate, to dictate terms, to exact tribute.

Because Jesus' body slumped without breath or heartbeat on a cross, death has no more power. He has risen from the tomb and continues to shout to our generation, "I am alive forevermore and have the keys of hell and death!"

The very fact of His life is verification that death is a vanquished foe. And in giving His life to us He provides a force in our lives to dominate death in all of its manifestations.

• How many live life in a casket of circumstances?

• How many tread through life up a gravelike rut?

• How many are tangled in the graveclothes of past experiences or habit?

Hear this! To you Christ comes and says, "Fear not! The

end of that which has come upon you is near at hand! What you feared would never change is shortly to be overthrown forever!"

I visited recently with a friend, an excellent pastor I've known since college days. A long season of frustration had weakened and depleted him, and when temptation came on strong, he fell.

Crushed and deeply humiliated by his failure, he left the ministry and moved his family to another city. He sought solace in the mountains. He bent his back to hard labor in an attempt to forget. He doubted the possibility of ever again realizing what he knew to be his life's God-ordained purpose.

Then, just when it seemed recovery had begun, a new dimension of depression engulfed him. At that point, he asked if we could get together to talk.

As we began to converse, a strange thing happened.

A vivid picture came into my mind — like a short video clip. I saw a pitch-black tunnel, stretching for miles beneath an enormous Everest of a mountain. I could see my friend groping along through the tunnel, feeling his way forward in the dark. Tears filled his eyes — as though he believed the mountain to be eternal and his "tunneling" endless. But somehow I could see that only a few feet of the dark, mountain tunnel remained! He was about to break through into the daylight!

I looked at my friend and said, "Jim, let me describe your feeling and your thinking." Then I related the picture and identified his sense of futility with the prospect that nothing would ever be any different.

"Jim," I told him, "you're almost through this! You have only a few feet to go. Don't despair. The Lord is wanting you to know that He has taken all futility out of your life-prospect. Things *will* change. The breakthrough is not far away!"

And Jim wept.

After some time he regained his composure. "Jack," he said, "I don't know how to thank God for those words. The darkness of my soul has been by itself enough to kill hope. But what has been the most destructive to me — robbing my life of any joy — was the thought, *Nothing will ever change.* But I know that's a lie. And God's truth has set me free to believe and to hope with certainty!"

In only a few weeks that hope was fulfilled. Jim did indeed break through the heavy darkness of depression and experienced a fresh release of life and light.

But Jim's real breakthrough began weeks before his depression lifted. It began when he caught a vision for the Lord's guaranteed victory in his life. It began when he gripped the live power line of resurrection life, and the fear of futility and death was broken. His response in faith was not the result of human wisdom or counsel. It was the Holy Spirit Himself bearing witness to the greatest counsel mankind can ever know:

Jesus Christ has broken the power of death to rule you at any point in your life.

The hope of your calling, the high destiny that God has for you, is realizable through the resurrection power of Jesus. The awesome power that raised Him from the dead is the same power that says, "I'm going to bring you through this."

Don't give a hearing to those shadows that come against you. Don't open the door to those fears that cause you to feel despair, discouragement, and defeat. And when those lying voices want to get you on the line and say, "You can't live with this anymore," hang up the phone! How often we listen to the bombardment of that garbage from hell rather than to our Lord who says, "I have high plans for you."

God has great plans for you. He has a high purpose for you. That's what it means in Ephesians 1:18 when Paul prays that we "may know the hope of His calling."

Where are you right now? Under a mountain in a long tunnel? Are you worse off than the scene after Calvary, when they took the broken, lifeless body of Jesus off the Cross? How hopeless can a scene be?

But Easter Sunday changed all that…forever. Since the bands of death have been broken, nothing can trap you. You can't be caught in a vise from which there is no release, nor bound in a yoke from which there is no deliverance.

The power of death has been broken. The rule of death has been nullified. You're already out of the tunnel…and it's a glorious morning!

> If death got the upper hand through one man's wrongdoing, can you imagine the breathtaking recovery life makes, sovereign life, in those who grasp with both hands this wildly extravagant life-gift, this grand setting-everything-right, that the one man Jesus Christ provides? (Romans 5:17, The Message)

I Believe in the Resurrection

"I am the resurrection and the life. . . .
Do you believe this?"

JOHN 11:26

I believe in the resurrection of Jesus Christ, the Son of God — that He personally, physically, and actually died and on the third day rose again according to the Scriptures. I believe that by His resurrection He declared His deity and announced His conquest of death and hell, and that all who believe this in their heart may be saved.

Because I believe this, I confess with my mouth the Lord Jesus and worship Him whom I glorify as the Son of God, risen from the grave and ascended upon high in triumph above all the powers of darkness.

I believe in the resurrection of the just, that at Christ's coming we shall all be changed into the likeness of His glorious, resurrected body. I believe we shall receive eternal, physical bodies which shall not be subject to decay, and in that glorified state we shall forever be with and serve the living God.

Because I believe this, I live life in hope of the resurrection, with-out fear of death and without bondage to the endless grieving of those who have no such hope.

I believe in the resurrection of all mankind, that on the last day every creature shall stand before the throne of God and give account for the deeds done in the body. I believe that by His death and resurrection, Christ Jesus has made it possible for every man, woman, and child to anticipate that day with joy, but that all those resistant to His Lordship shall experience endless judgment in bodies intended to know eternal blessing rather than eternal shame.

Because I believe this, I walk in faith and holy sobriety, knowing that my motives as well as my deeds, my thoughts as well as my words constitute the substance of eternal values which I either serve or shirk and according to which I shall be judged before the loving and righteous Father.

With such an expectation as this, I can walk in praise to a resurrected Savior who has not only given me an eternal hope but who can fill me with an eternal quality of life and power to live daily in the resources of His victory.

The Best and Final Word

"Go quickly and tell His disciples that
He has risen from the dead."

MATTHEW 28:7

hirty-nine years ago, in a little church in Indiana, I celebrated my first Easter as a pastor. The morning was memorable for at least two reasons.

First, until that morning, I'd never had the privilege of leading God's people to the Empty Tomb. Our numbers were small that morning as we worshiped the Risen One…but our joy was great.

Second, it was my first Easter as a father! In the wee hours of that Easter morning, our firstborn child came into the world. How much joy can one sleepy, new preacher-daddy contain?

As I was greeting the departing congregation at the door that morning, an elderly brother named Walter took my hand in both of his big, work-roughened hands. Walter had recently emigrated from Germany. He had a thick accent and a big smile.

"Pastor," he said, "I vant to tell you somezing. In Germany, ve haf a greeting on Easter Sunday, und I vant to teach it to you, yah?"

"Of course, Walter," I said.

"Vell," he told me, "one person says, 'Christ is risen!' Und ze other person says, 'He is risen indeed!'"

I thanked my elderly friend and said good-bye. But I didn't forget! Every Easter since that morning, I've lead gatherings of God's people in that statement and reply.

But right now, right here…it's just you and me. Will you join me, wherever you are, in that declaration? Put your heart into it, friend. And more, put your *life* into it. There is no more important truth in earth or heaven, in time or eternity. Say it with me…

Christ is risen!
HE IS RISEN INDEED!

A Final Thought

from Pastor Jack Hayford

To build a bridge across a deep, impassable chasm...?

It begins with a single cable. A line is stretched from one side of the chasm to the other, and once the two sides of the canyon have been joined, everything builds from there.

It's done easily today. Stretching such a cable is child's play for a helicopter. But great, even majestic, bridges were built across seemingly bottomless distances well before the days of airplanes and helicopters.

How was it done?

I came across a historical article recently which helped lay that mystery to rest. The engineers in this account were faced with a huge crevasse, extremely deep and over five hundred yards across. What did they do? They rolled a huge cannon to one edge of the ravine, attached a thin cable to a cannonball, and fired it across the chasm to the other side.

It worked! Beginning with one thin cable stretched across

that yawning fissure, a great bridge would eventually be constructed and then traversed by countless people through the years.

That picture came to mind one day as I was studying Jesus' words from the Cross. In His darkest moment, He cried out, *"My God, My God, why have You forsaken Me?"*

In fact, at that very instant, He was being hurled across a chasm — vast, infinitely wide, and impossibly deep. Because of the guilt and shame of your sin and mine, He was thrust out and away from the presence of our holy God, the Father who doubtless felt the pain of that separation as much as His Son did. His Son was, and is, mankind's only Savior — Jesus, who came to earth and lived in loving and sinless perfection. And so it was, when all our sin had been laid on Him, He was "shot" across that chasm of hopelessness like that cannonball attached to the cable. In that one act He spanned the infinite distance that not one person among all humanity — none of us! — could ever bridge in a trillion years of reaching and stretching. He, who from eternity past had enjoyed perfect fellowship with His Father, willingly allowed Himself to be separated from Him for that moment. He was hurled across the great gulf into the depths of death and hell — for us!

But on that resurrection morning our Jesus came out of the grave. With one side of the "line" secured on earth, He ascended to His Father in the highest heaven. That was both the beginning of the great bridge and the beginning of the great parade...from our "sin and death" unto God's forgiveness and eternal life.

The procession continues.

Where once there was only black distance and endless space, a majestic bridge now arches over the terrible depths: from hell to heaven, from despair to hope, from death to life, from eternal darkness to God's everlasting kingdom of light. Millions have already crossed to the other side, and the way is still open for you and me.

The bridge He desired to build, though it cost Him His blood and life, is now completed, and we are wise never to forget the prayer He prayed as He approached His Cross:

"Father, I desire that they also whom You gave me may be with Me where I am, that they may behold My glory which You have given Me; for You loved Me before the foundation of the world."
(John 17:24)

Each Easter, we celebrate the Father's glorious answer to the Son's "glory" prayer that brought the resurrection's glorious morning. The bridge is complete. It may be narrow — eternal life comes through Jesus alone — but it *is* secure. No person or power in earth, heaven, or hell can shake it.

At our end of the bridge, two great signs point the way. One says:

"I am the way, the truth, and the life. No one comes to the Father except through Me." (John 14:6)

The other reads:

"He who hears My word and believes in Him who sent Me has everlasting life, and shall not come into judgment but has passed from death into life." (John 5:24)

- All sin has been paid for!
- Death's power has been broken!
- Hell's gates have been shattered!
- Futility has been bypassed!

The bridge is open — straight through to the highest heaven.

And to choose to cross it, dear friend, is to know that your eternal life begins that very day. So *do* make that choice…please. I have, and I guarantee you…

It *is* glorious!

Jack Hayford

Notes

Notes

Notes

Notes

Notes

Notes

Notes

Notes